WATCHING YOUR BACK
Injury Prevention for Junior Athletes

WATCHING YOUR BACK
Injury Prevention for Junior Athletes

Michael Chang, TPI Certified   Gerry Chang

With a Foreword by Dr. Michael Hollstegge

Notice

This book is intended as a reference volume only, not as a medical manual. The information given here is designed to help you make informed decisions about your health. It is not intended as a substitute for professional medical advice. If you have a medical problem, we urge you to seek competent medical help.

The authors have made every effort to ensure the accuracy of the information within this book. However, the information in this book is not intended to serve as a replacement for proper exercise training. Any use of the information in this book is at the reader's discretion. The authors and publisher disclaim any and all liability arising directly or indirectly from the use or application of any information contained in this book. A healthcare professional should be consulted regarding your specific condition.

Table of Contents

Foreword 2

Introduction 5

Part 1: My Backstory 6

Part 2: Important Exercises 14

Part 3: Injury Prevention Tips 24

Part 4: Golf Swing Faults 66

Part 5: Mental Game 76

References 84

Foreword

My career as a doctor of physical therapy has exposed me to the gamut of sports injuries. When a young person suffers an injury while on the playing field, the trauma involves both body and mind. The athlete's body, giving greater rewards through greater experience and training, suddenly fails to function as it once did. Even more distressing, the non-compliant body part is seized with pain--an unwelcome sensation to anyone, but particularly frightening to a teenager.

That brings me to Michael Chang. This avid young golfer came to me after a professional diagnosis of a spinal injury directly connected to his golfing. From his first visit, I saw an optimistic and confident young man. Michael didn't show inner doubt or frustration, but I knew it was there. How? Because I had been in Michael's shoes at his same age. A sports enthusiast with my sights set on joining my high school basketball team, I was devastated when I tore a hamstring. Would I ever run again, let alone be on a basketball court? I asked myself in despair.

My doctor sent me to a physical therapist. After several sessions, my hamstring had recovered so well that I made the basketball team in time for the season's start. That experience gave me an appreciation of physical therapists and opened my eyes to the valuable work they do in improving the quality of people's lives. It also led to my decision to go to college and obtain a doctorate degree in Physical Therapy.

Thus, Michael's injury was more than bodily harm. I had to understand the "story" his body was telling me. Each athlete's story is unique. And in my first sessions with Michael, we were able to break the injury down and agree upon a treatment plan. The first solution, then, was not to put a hypothetical bandage on the problem, but to work through Michael's physical assets and deficits, gradually finding functional activities that could be managed safely and sensibly. Moreover, since I share Michael's dedication to golf, I was even able to offer Michael suggestions for changing his golf swing and other movements while playing.

One day, Michael and his brother Gerry came to me with the idea of writing a book to help their peer group, twelve to eighteen year olds, avoid athletic injuries by detailing some of the exercises and techniques Michael had learned in physical therapy. I was impressed. After recovering from his own injury, Michael's first thought was to use his own experiences to benefit other people. The book was not an ego trip for the young man, but a sincere desire to help others.

Wisely, Michael and Gerry have chosen to focus on prevention rather than rehabilitation from sports injuries. From Michael's own experience, he has deduced the valuable lesson that a single injury prevented is worth ten injuries from which one recovers, requiring numerous (and costly) sessions at the physical therapist's office.

It has been inspiring watching their efforts in creating this book. I have combed through and validated the exercises as well as what they are in here to work on improving. And it is with professional and personal pride that I give my full support to all aspects of this book.

Watching Your Back is especially aimed at those young men and women between the ages of twelve and eighteen engaged in non-contact sports: golf, baseball, tennis, rowing, weight lifting, gymnastics, among others. I think this book is instrumental for these young athletes to read and understand the importance of taking care of their bodies to promote the longevity of their athletic careers. Meanwhile, this book can still be very important for those not in this age group, such as parents and other adults in general.

I strongly recommend everyone to read this book.

Dr. Michael Hollstegge, PT, DPT, CAFS, TPI-CGI
Co-Founder and CEO of ReKinected Physical Therapy
www.rekinectedpt.com

Introduction

This book is recommended for young athletes between the ages of 12 and 18 playing golf or other non-contact sports. However, it is still useful for all ages since back injuries are exceedingly common (one such condition called spondylolisthesis affects up to 7% of the total population!).

Aside from my personal experience, I did a lot of research (see reference books at the end), and I am Titleist Performance Institute (TPI) Certified. I hope that you will find this book helpful when playing the sport you love. Are you ready to learn how to reduce your chances of injuring yourself? Turn the page and away we go!

Part 1: My Backstory

"An ounce of prevention is worth a pound of cure." If you haven't heard this expression yet, at some point in your life, I guarantee you will. It was coined by Benjamin Franklin, the great American inventor, statesman and not incidentally, the man whose face appears on every hundred dollar bill.

Basically, Franklin said that, when dealing with a problem, spending a small amount of time and effort early on is a good investment. It will save you a lot more trouble in the long run. And, getting back to those crispy "Ben Franklins," it'll save your parents a lot of money too.

Similarly, this idea also applies to your sports career. I learned that lesson from the wonderful thing called hindsight. With back injuries (or injuries in general) being extremely common even in young athletes, I feel that it is very important for everyone to be aware of these risks and how to avoid them when starting sports. Athletics are very important for many people as they offer potential career paths, hobbies, and health benefits. However, sports aren't exactly good for your health if they cause injuries. The question, then, is how can you have a beneficial sports experience without suffering the setbacks that injuries create?

I've always loved sports. I started playing golf competitively when I was 12. Before that, I had played soccer for six years. I had an amazing soccer career in which I scored some goals, got kicked a lot, became the team captain, pretended to be hurt, got a yellow card after someone else pretended to be hurt, and won some tournaments. I played for FC Heat, a soccer club in Escondido, California. FC Heat is a nonprofit organization that reaches into the community to include kids of every race and economic level.

After six years, though, I was ready for a change, so I switched to a non-contact sport--golf. Soccer had taught me to be a team player, a valuable skill, but through golf, I believed that I would learn the additional lessons of patience, discipline and self-reliance.

But my new sport brought two lessons I had not anticipated. The first was pain. The second was recovery.

The start was a minor annoyance with a little pain in my lower back after a year of playing golf competitively. When I went to a doctor, I was told that it was just ordinary muscle pains that were common among young golfers. With that major crisis overcome (or so I thought), I continued along my golf career hoping that the worst was behind me. Turns out, that was a bad idea.

Feeling reassured from the doctor's words, I decided to begin intensive golf training in Florida. Not only was the training intense, so was the pain in my back. At one point, it hurt so much to swing a club that I couldn't execute full swings for weeks at a time. Still, my caring parents and I kept thinking the problem was the mild muscle pain all athletes feel. Once again, that turned out to be a bad idea.

Dismissing the pain, I continued my golf training. Then the pain became even worse. It started as a dull ache deep in my back, but after a few months, it had begun radiating down the side of my right leg. When half swings were all I could manage during entire tournaments, I realized it was time to seek another doctor. This time, the doctor ordered an X-ray. It came back showing I had no problems. "What a relief!" I naively thought. Turns out, that would be a very bad idea (you probably see some repeated themes going on).

Soon afterwards, as I bent down to pick up something off the floor, I felt a sharp pain shooting through my lower back. It hurt to move so much that I couldn't even straighten up or walk without help. Bedridden for a few days, I had to withdraw from a big tournament I'd been preparing for. I was disappointed, to say the least.

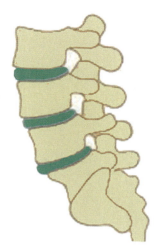

Healthy spine

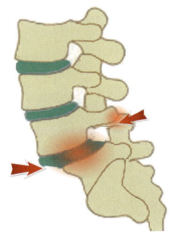

Spondylolisthesis

It was off to another doctor, a sports medicine specialist, who gave me another diagnosis. This time, I was given not just another X-ray but an MRI (magnetic resonance imaging) scan as well.

Back in the doctor's office, I got some sobering news. I had a spinal condition called spondylolisthesis (pronounced spohn-di-low-less-THEE-sis). Spondylolisthesis occurs when a piece of your vertebra (bone in your spine) is fractured, causing an instability in this section of your spine. In my case, they are called stress fractures because the fractures happened due to repetitive motions from my golf swing that constantly stressed my back. Consequently, the vertebra slips out of place, putting pressure on nerve roots and generally being a pain in the… well… back.

Spondylolisthesis occurs for many reasons. Some people are born with it. In my case, the fracture to my spinal joints were due to the repeated motions of my swinging a golf club.

I must have looked shocked at getting my diagnosis. However, the doctor quickly reassured me that my case was relatively mild. Still, as spinal injuries go, it must have been developing slowly for years.

You may be asking, Well, if the condition had been developing for some time, why hadn't it been caught by my initial X-ray? Unfortunately, X-rays can't detect problems 100 percent of the time. And they're especially bad at catching stress fractures.

The doctor also told me that spondylolisthesis is not unusual: up to 7 percent of the population experiences this. Later on, after researching the condition, I found out that many people with spondylolisthesis don't even know they have it--that is, until symptoms manifest. Moreover, spondylolisthesis is very common among young athletes playing sports involving a lot of spinal rotation. Golf, naturally, is one of these.

My problem could be treated in two ways. One was surgery which might help the spinal bones from shifting, but there was no guarantee of a full, pain-free recovery. The other option was three to nine months of no sports but regular sessions of physical therapy to build muscle around my spine to support it, making the pain more tolerable but still not completely solving the issue.

I chose physical therapy, and after several months, I was feeling much stronger, though the result was not perfect. Now, I am starting to get back into golf and even some tournaments. The pain hasn't disappeared, but I now know how to avoid unnecessarily stressing the lower back joints.

That is my story (or my backstory, if you will). After doing a lot of research, meeting with countless doctors, physical therapists, and coaches, I still struggle with this problem but have learned a lot of important lessons.

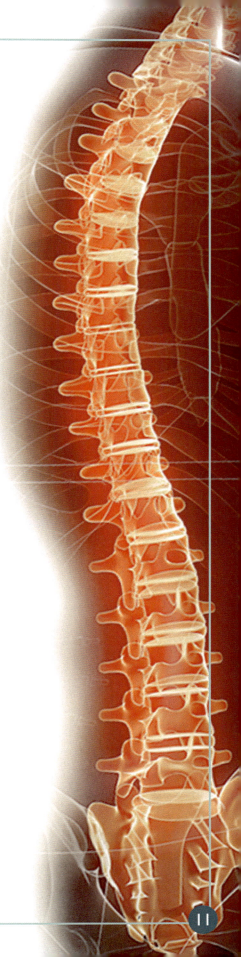

The idea for this book came to me when I was working through a long and arduous recovery with my physical therapist. My brother, who has been a great source of encouragement and comfort throughout my recovery, became very excited about my idea. We decided to write the book together because he knew my entire experience with playing golf, and he helped and supported me tremendously through this project.

With this book I hope to raise awareness about back injuries among young athletes competing in non-contact sports. I want to offer advice that I wish I had known, such as how you should practice, what exercises can help prevent injuries, when you should see a doctor and/or get an X-ray or MRI, and many more of the possible difficulties you may face. I cannot emphasize enough how crucial injury prevention is; it is always better to avoid injuries than to have to go through the strenuous process of recovering (which may not even be possible in some cases).

I would like to clarify that having back conditions (whether you were born with it or you detected it early) does not mean that you should not participate in sports, such as golf, baseball, tennis, rowing, weight lifting, gymnastics, and such. Rather, it just means that you have to take extra precautions and know your limits so your injury is not worsened by your athletic activities. I have seen many fellow golfers and young athletes who injure themselves and have to face major setbacks due to the mistakes they made--mistakes that were similar to mine. It is a common misconception that sports like golf don't have risks, so it is easy to think that injury prevention is unimportant. I hope to prevent other young athletes from facing the same problems I did. This book is an accumulation of my experiences in dealing with injuries, what mistakes I made, and how you can avoid those mistakes to have a much higher chance of having a fun, beneficial, and injury-free sports career.

And if you're injured and can't play for a while? Well, maybe that great Yankees manager, Joe Torre said it best: "Winning doesn't come from constant competition. It comes from preparation, courage, understanding heart and nurturing yourself. Winning is the result."

Part 2: Injury Prevention Tips

If injury prevention is the most important thing when working with non-contact sports, what is the best way to prevent injuries? Based on my experience, the first step would be to get a back X-ray and/or MRI before you even start golf (or any other non-contact sport where back injuries are common). Some conditions, such as spondylolisthesis, can be present before you even start a sport. An X-ray or MRI will let you know if it is safe to do so. I know it sounds like a lot and seems unnecessary, but it's always better to not take the risk. After all, if you do have this condition (or others like it), it will cause many more difficulties.

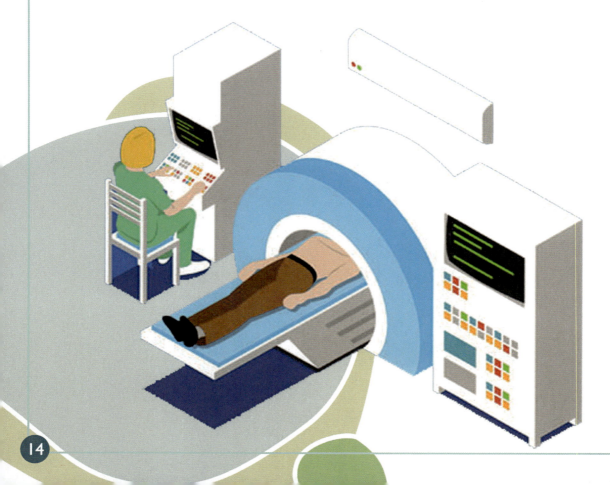

After I was diagnosed, I had to stop playing competitive golf and do months of physical therapy, and I will have to deal with this problem for the rest of my life. You can never be too cautious when it comes to injury prevention. It is not worth it to get into a sport unaware about a spinal condition you have and be forced to stop. Get an X-ray or even an MRI beforehand (remember, X-rays may not always catch the issue).

I would also like to note that if you do find a back injury from a preemptive MRI and/or X-ray, it does not mean that you cannot play golf (or whatever sport you are choosing). You can still play, but you must be extra cautious and put even more emphasis on the injury prevention stretches and warmups (I will go over some basic ones later).

But what happens if you do get injured when playing? Almost all players suffer from mild injuries that don't turn out to be a big deal. How do you know what is a major back injury and what is not? Muscle injuries are quite common and aren't too big of a deal, but spinal injuries could potentially be serious. How do you know if you should see a doctor?

First of all, it never hurts to see a doctor just in case. You definitely want to catch injuries early and before they get worse. Based on my experience and after talking to many doctors and physical therapists, here is what I would recommend you do if you hurt yourself while playing non-contact sports like golf. I will focus on what to do if you are a golfer, but these steps can be easily applied to other sports as well (such as baseball, tennis, rowing, ect.). Work your way down the list until either you recover or a problem is discovered and addressed.

Steps to take if you get hurt (especially if it is a back injury):

Step 1: Stop

If you feel pain from performing a certain motion such as a golf swing, stop and give yourself a minute or two to readjust. Then, take two or three more swings, and if it still hurts, take a break.

stop and give yourself a minute to **readjust**

Step 2: Resume

Try to resume after a brief rest. If it still hurts, then make sure to stop and take the rest of the day off, or work on other things that don't strain your back so much (like chipping and putting). If the pain is gone, venture forth cautiously. The crisis may have been averted. If the pain doesn't go away, move onto the next step.

Step 3: Recover

Do the following when you get home:

1. Ice the injured area for the first 24 hours (do this for about 15-20 minutes every 2-3 hours) until the pain recedes.
2. If your muscles are tight after the ice, use heat (for 15-20 minutes every 2-3 hours).
3. Icing and heating may cause you to be stiff afterwards, so lightly stretch **and foam roll (I will go into more detail about these later. Turn to Part 3, "Important Exercises," for these). Do not do any workouts.**

This may solve the problem, but if the pain does not improve after 48 hours (this is the key), continue to the next step.

Step 4: Assess

Identify the pain and go see a doctor. When I first got injured, I thought it was nothing and kept playing. That was a big mistake. It never hurts to see a doctor and you should definitely do so if the pain doesn't improve after 48 hours. It is also important to identify what kind of pain you are feeling. Although you are most likely not a trained professional and can't diagnose yourself, most doctors advise you to watch out for these symptoms if you feel pain in your lower back:

1. Shooting/sharp/stabbing pain

Could be a serious problem. It may be a spinal injury, especially if the pain goes down your leg. Be very cautious.

2. Sore/pulling/throbbing pain

Probably a muscle strain, but it still doesn't hurt to see a doctor.

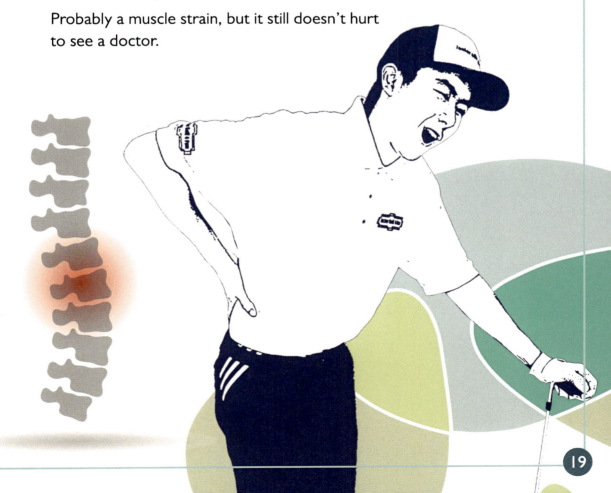

Step 5: (see a) Doctor

See a doctor, especially if you feel that the pain is going down your leg (though they will probably ask anyway). This piece of information is important to tell your doctor. Most doctors and physical therapists use the type of pain you're experiencing as a guideline to diagnose and treat the injury. The doctors will tell you if an X-ray or any further actions are required.

Step 6: Observe

This may be the most important step. If you have gotten this far, it means you hurt yourself and the pain continued even after taking a break. You took the proper measures to recover, but that didn't work, so you saw a doctor. The doctor checked you out and said you were okay. You made sure to rest, and now you are back to practicing.

Now, you need to keep an eye on your injury. You may think everything is okay as you went to a doctor and/or got an X-ray, but that is exactly the mistake I made. When I went to the doctor, I got an X-ray, but it didn't catch the problem. As a result, I wrongfully assumed that the pain was normal and that if I felt it again, it was no big deal. Even if the X-ray doesn't find any problems, do not immediately assume everything is okay. Ease yourself back into your normal practice routine; do not push yourself beyond your limits. If you find the pain is still persistent, go see the doctor again or get a second opinion from another medical expert.

The Bottom Line...

All of this may seem overwhelming, but what I can't emphasize enough is the importance of prevention over curing. There are no guaranteed ways to prevent injuries, and the same can be said for curing them. We must try and improve the probability of catching injuries early on so they don't get worse in the future and bring even more problems. Get a preemptive X-ray or MRI and follow these steps: Stop, Resume, Recover, Assess, (visit a) Doctor, and Observe. If you get hurt, work your way down the list of steps which create an amazing and easy to remember acronym: SRRA-DO. Take injuries seriously. When you feel pain, it is your body trying to tell you something. Don't ignore it.

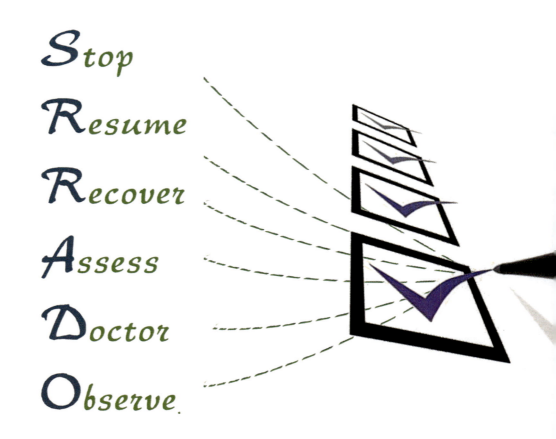

Stop

Resume

Recover

Assess

Doctor

Observe

Part 3: Important Exercises

In preventing or relieving pain from lower back injuries, the most important aspects to focus on are lower body and core strength, as well as flexibility. Lower back injuries generally have a few different causes. One possibility is tightness in the lower body muscles, such as your quads, hamstrings, hips, glutes, etc. Tightness in those muscles could cause your lower back to need to compensate by moving in ways that it is not supposed to, which can lead to injury. Another potential cause of back injuries is core or lower body weakness. If your core and lower body are not strong enough, your lower back may have to compensate or move more than it should when you are performing different actions or athletic activities. Given these points, we need to ensure that we have both sufficient flexibility and strength in your core and lower body to support your lower back. So, let's get into some good exercises to achieve these goals.

This chapter has organized many exercises into different sections. I will talk about how to perform them and give important tips and notes about each exercise. Moreover, I will also give some suggestions on how to organize your schedule and when to perform the exercises in each section.

If you flipped to this section because you are using your SRRADO checklist and you need to relieve some pain from a back injury (you should be on step 3, "Recover"), you're in the right section. Mainly focus on all the stretches/exercises under "Important Stretches," "Michael's Warm-Up Routine," and "Foam Rolling Exercises." I would not recommend you perform any exercises in "Strengthening Exercises" if you are injured. Just stretch, foam roll, and rest. Continue forth with your SRRADO checklist and I wish you a speedy recovery.

Without further ado, let us begin our journey of exterminating injuries.

Foam Rolling:

Before stretching, you should foam roll. Imagine a rubber band with a knot in it. Is it easier to stretch the rubber band with the knot or when you untie the knot? Obviously, when you untie the knot. Foam rolling essentially does that with your muscles, loosening them up to make them easier to stretch. To foam roll, you will need… a foam roller. They come in different firmness levels. When starting out, I recommend using one that is relatively softer because foam rolling can cause your muscles to feel sore (especially if you are tight or have never done it before), but that is normal. It will also help relieve muscle pains, so if you ever feel pain in a muscle, try to foam roll it.

If you've never tried foam rolling before, the basic idea is that you place the foam roller on the ground and lay the muscle you want to roll on the roller. Then move your body back and forth along the roller so it can loosen up that area. It is similar to a massage. Pressure is applied along certain muscles to soften them up, which can help with flexibility and relieve tension and pain (although you might feel a little bit sore when it's happening). Foam rolling may sound complicated but it's pretty simple once you see it. Look at the pictures and descriptions and you will understand.

 The yellow dots show you what part of your body we are foam rolling or stretching.

Calves:

Step 1: Set up with your hands and one foot on the ground. Then place the calf of your other leg on the foam roller and lift yourself up.

Step 2: Move back and forth along the roller by pushing with your hands and the foot that is on the ground. The roller should be rolling along your entire calf, which helps the muscle loosen up.

Step 3: For a more intense variation, place one leg on top of your other calf. This is to put more weight on the calf that you are rolling in order to get a more vigorous exercise. When starting out, you don't need to do this. You can instead perform the less intense version above.

Step 4: Roll each calf five times (five times back and forth).

Hamstring:

Step 1: This exercise is similar to rolling your calves, but instead of the foam roller being under your calves, it is under your hamstrings.

Step 2: Once again, push with your hands to move your entire hamstring along the foam roller. To get a more intense roll, put more weight on your leg by placing one leg over the one you are rolling. Of course, if it is too difficult to do this, you can start out by not putting one leg on top of the other.

Step 3: Roll each hamstring five times (five times back and forth).

Quads:

Step 1: To roll your quads, set up on your stomach, with your hands under your chest and your quad on the roller.

Step 2: Lift up and support yourself with your arms and other leg.

Step 3: Push your body back and forth with your arms and your leg that is the ground. Roll the foam roller along your entire quad.

Step 4: Roll each quad five times (five back and forth).

IT Band:

Step 1: To roll your IT band, set up on your side, with your lower leg straightened and your IT band on the foam roller. Use your hands and one leg to support yourself.

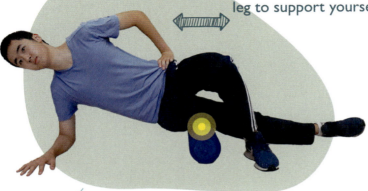

Step 2: To move yourself along the roller, push with your arms and the foot that is on the ground. Roll the foam roller along your entire IT band.

Step 3: Roll each IT band five times (five back and forth).

Glutes:

Step 1: To foam roll your glutes, cross one leg onto your other knee and sit on the foam roller while leaning on the glute of the crossed leg. The reason you bring one leg onto the other knee is to expose that side's glute muscles and get a stronger roll.

Step 2: Roll each glute five times (five back and forth).

T-Spine:

- Step 1: To roll out your T-spine (thoracic spine), lie down with your upper back on the roller.

 - Step 2: Lift your body up off the ground, and place your hands behind your head.

 - Step 3: Push with your feet and roll out your upper back. Do this five times (five back and forth).

Another Important Note About Foam Rolling:

It is also very important that you not only foam roll before stretching but also after a day of sports practice or a workout. Foam rolling all your muscles will help you relax. This step is very important when it comes to injury prevention, so don't skip it. I understand that it can be annoying to do this every day after practice, but relaxing your muscles after practice will not only help prevent injuries but also help you recover from muscle pains faster. Foam rolling your whole body only takes a couple minutes and doing it every day can bring many benefits, so don't forget to do it or else… I'll be very sad.

Important Stretches:

When you are stretching, make sure that you move slowly and carefully. Oftentimes, people will both move into and lift out of a stretch too quickly, or try to push themselves too far past their limit. These mistakes can all get you a free ticket to Injuryland, so instead, make sure that you are performing every stretch slowly and gradually. Stretching can be uncomfortable, but if it becomes painful, then stretch less intensely. Listen to your body.

An important thing to note about these stretches is that they are known as static stretches. This means that doing them does not require a lot of motion. Some experts suggest that you don't do these stretches before working out.

Additionally, if you are here because you were injured and are following your SRRADO list, do these stretches, but less vigorously than usual. Stop if these stretches, for any reason, cause your injury to become painful. If such is the case, move to Step 4 of SRRADO.

Now we shall move onward with the stretching. Here are the stretches that I do. I like to work from the bottom up, so I start with my lower body and then move onto my upper body.

Calves:

Step 1: Find a wall or something you can lean against for this stretch.

Step 2: Stand a foot or two from the wall, facing it.

Step 3: Step one leg backward so you are in a bit of a split-squat stance, and place your hands at about shoulder-height on the wall.

Step 4: Bend your front knee and bring your chest and hips toward the wall, using your hands to support yourself. Keep the heel of your back foot flat on the ground. You should feel a stretch in the calf of your back leg.

Step 5: You can control the intensity of the stretch by varying how much you lean into the wall. Hold for 30 seconds, then switch sides.

Hamstrings:

- Step 1: Standing on one foot, prop the other foot up on something at around knee-height (maybe a chair or bench).

- Step 2: Bend forward and reach for the toe of the leg that is propped up. Try not to hunch over from your upper back when reaching forward. Instead, bend more from the hip and keep your upper back flat.

- Step 3: Hold for 30 seconds, then switch sides.

Quads (flamingo stretch):

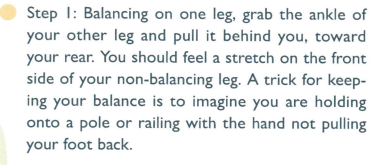

Step 1: Balancing on one leg, grab the ankle of your other leg and pull it behind you, toward your rear. You should feel a stretch on the front side of your non-balancing leg. A trick for keeping your balance is to imagine you are holding onto a pole or railing with the hand not pulling your foot back.

Step 2: Hold for 30 seconds, then switch sides.

Kneeling Hip Flexor Stretch:

Step 1: Start by getting down on one knee and making sure your chest and hips all face forward.

Step 2: Shift your weight forward. You should feel a stretch on the hip of the leg with the knee on the ground.

Step 3: The important thing to remember with this stretch is to keep your back from arching when you shift forward. To prevent this, tighten your core by feeling like you're pulling your navel in toward your spine. In doing so, you may also feel a stronger stretch in your hip.

Step 4: Hold for 30 seconds, then switch sides.

Glutes/Piriformis:

- Step 1: Lie down on the floor on your back.
- Step 2: Place your right foot on your left knee.
- Step 3: Then, pull your left leg back toward your chest. You should feel a stretch in your right glute and piriformis.

- Step 4: Hold for 30 seconds, then switch sides.

Shoulders (elephant stretch):

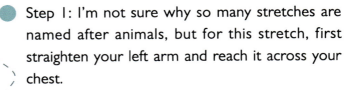

- Step 1: I'm not sure why so many stretches are named after animals, but for this stretch, first straighten your left arm and reach it across your chest.
- Step 2: Bend your right arm and cross it over your left arm.
- Step 3: Using your right arm, pull your left arm toward your chest and to the right.
- Step 4: Hold for 30 seconds, then switch sides.

Michael's Warm-up Routine:

This is the warm-up routine I go through before I golf or work out. If you play a sport other than golf, you may have your own warm-up routine, but it may be useful to add these exercises to your routine. We need to make sure that our muscles are prepared to perform athletically and have the necessary range of motion to do so. You can also do these exercises if your back is hurting. Just perform them less vigorously and stop if they cause more pain.

To warm up, I do dynamic exercises to get everything moving. If possible, foam roll before doing these exercises because doing so softens your muscles and helps you warm up more quickly. If you do not have a foam roller with you, you can also walk around or jog, just to get moving a little.

When doing dynamic exercises, people often perform them very quickly and jerkily, which could (you guessed it) lead to injuries. Instead, perform every movement in a controlled manner.

Once again, to those who flipped to this section due to the fact that you suffered an injury and are following your SRRADO checklist, do these exercises very carefully and much less vigorously than usual. Stop if they cause you pain for any reason.

5-Way Hip Flexor Stretch:

This is a dynamic variation of the hip flexor stretch, and while the exercise does stretch your hips, it also stretches your groin muscles.

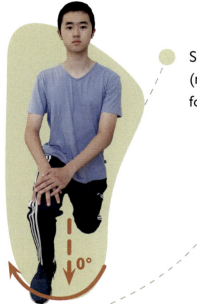

Step 1: Start by getting down on your left knee (note: your left leg will stay planted in that position for the entire stretch).

Step 2: Lean forward and perform the standard hip flexor stretch, but only hold for about two to three seconds, then straighten back up to center.

Step 3: Keeping your left knee on the ground and your hips facing forward, move your right leg 45 degrees to the right. Now, lean into your right leg with the same movement as the standard hip flexor stretch. This time, because your right leg is offset, you will feel a stretch more in the front left groin muscle. Hold for two to three seconds, then come back to center.

- Step 4: Move your right leg another 45 degrees to the right so that it forms a 90 degree angle with your left leg. You can allow your hip and chest to rotate a little with the right leg as you move it to the side, but your left leg needs to stay planted. Now, lean into your right leg again. This time, you should feel a stretch closer to the inner part of your left groin muscle. Hold for two to three seconds, then come back to center.

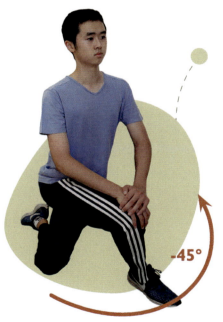

- Step 5: Move your right leg yet another 45 degrees to the right, so that it is now behind you. Allow your chest and hips to rotate with your right leg. Lean into the right leg. Now you should feel a stretch in the groin muscles of your legs. Hold for two to three seconds, then come back to center.

- Step 6: Bring your right leg back to the starting position, then across your left leg, turning it 45 degrees to the left this time. Now, lean into your right leg again, and this time you should feel a light stretch in the right glute. Hold for two to three seconds then come back to center.

- Step 7: For each leg, perform at least three sets of the above. This is a very good stretch for hip and groin mobility, which are essential for any kind of athletic activity. Furthermore, we are even doing a bit of lower body activation by constantly putting weight onto the front leg and changing directions.

Standing Glute/Piriformis Stretch:

- Step 1: Balance on one leg and lift your other foot and place it on the knee of your balancing leg. You may want to use a golf club or hold onto something to help you keep your balance.

- Step 2: Squat down and reach forward at the same time. You should feel a stretch in the glute of your non-balancing leg. Hold for two to three seconds, then come up, and repeat. You can try to reach in different directions as you stretch. For example, reach a bit more to the left the first time, then reach toward the middle another time, and then reach toward the right the third time. You will feel that the area of your glute being stretched varies a little depending on the direction you reach toward as you stretch.

- Step 3: Perform 6 reps per side.

Tilting Lunge:

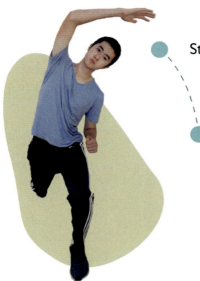

Step 1: Start by standing straight.

Step 2: Perform a basic forward lunge with your left leg (Remember, to keep your back from arching, tighten your core!).

Step 3: Once you are in that lunged position, reach your right arm over your head and bend to the left. You should feel a stretch in your right side, the side of your right hip, and maybe even a little in your right lower back. Make sure you are bending left only and not bending backward or forward (which could put pressure on your spine).

Step 4: Hold for two to three seconds, then straighten up and push out of your lunge. Alternating both sides, perform 6 reps per side. This is a good warm-up exercise because you are activating your lower body and maintaining balance as you tilt to the side, while simultaneously focusing on stretching your side.

Walking Hamstring Stretch:

- Step 1: Start by standing straight.

- Step 2: Step back with your right leg and squat backwards while reaching your hands forward and down toward the ground. Allow your left toe to come up while keeping your heel on the ground. Hold the stretch for about two to three seconds, then straighten up, and step backward with your left leg and perform the same stretch on the other leg. Perform 6 reps per leg. This is another good dynamic exercise that includes lower body activation, balance, and stretching.

Side Lunge Groin Stretch:

Step 1: Start by standing straight.

Step 2: Take a large step out to the left and sink down into a side lunge while raising both arms to shoulder width. You should feel a stretch in your groin muscle. Hold the stretch for about three seconds.

Step 3: Without lifting out of the lunge, shift your weight to your right and stretch the other side. Hold for two to three seconds.

Step 4: Come up and out of the lunge, this time step to the right, and repeat the stretch. Alternate sides and perform 6 reps per leg. This exercise includes more lower body activation and even some weight shift, which is crucial in the golf swing.

Step and reach:

- Step 1: Find the corner of a wall and stand with it to your right.

- Step 2: Place your right hand against the wall and step forward with your right foot.

- Step 3: As you step forward, reach your left hand forward, allowing your upper body to stretch and rotate to the right.

Use your right hand to support youself and to push away from the wall, which will give you a stronger stretch. Hold for about two to three seconds, then step back out of the stretch, and repeat. Perform 6 reps per side.

Step and reach golf club variation:

This stretch is very similar to the step and reach, but all we need is a golf club (or a stick of some sort) instead of the corner of a wall.

- Step 1: Place your hands at the ends of the golf club, holding the club with your hands palm-down. Raise the club up to shoulder-height.

- Step 2: Step forward with your right leg into almost a lunge, and rotate your upper body to the right. Hold for two to three seconds, then come up and switch sides.

Perform 6 reps per side. Now, in these two exercises, we are beginning to incorporate rotation into lower body activation, which is crucial in the golf swing and any rotational sports.

Step and rotate:

You will need a golf club or something similar for this exercise (like a stick).

Step 1: Place your hands at the ends of the golf club. Hold the club with your left hand palm-down and your right-hand palm up. Raise the club up to shoulder-height.

Step 2: Step forward with your left leg into almost a lunge, and rotate your upper body left and down, as if you were rowing a boat. Your upper body can lean forward a little to allow yourself to rotate in more of a downward direction, but make sure you keep your core tight. Hold for two to three seconds.

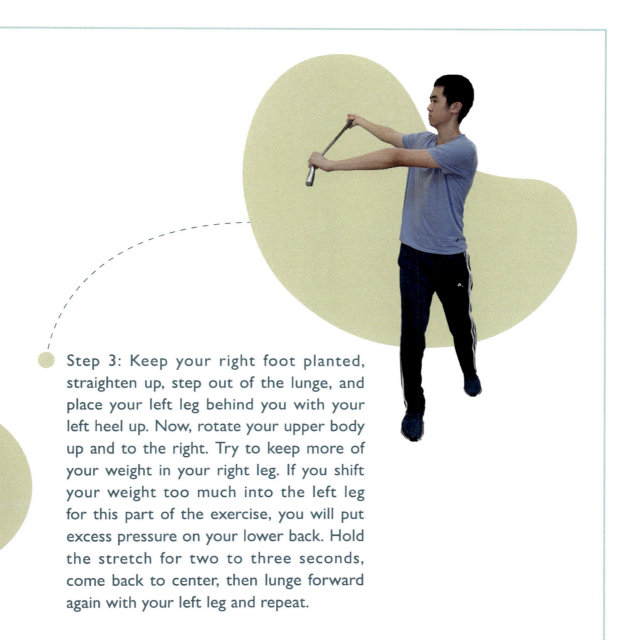

Step 3: Keep your right foot planted, straighten up, step out of the lunge, and place your left leg behind you with your left heel up. Now, rotate your upper body up and to the right. Try to keep more of your weight in your right leg. If you shift your weight too much into the left leg for this part of the exercise, you will put excess pressure on your lower back. Hold the stretch for two to three seconds, come back to center, then lunge forward again with your left leg and repeat.

Perform 6 reps with planting the left leg, then 6 reps with planting the right leg. This exercise is similar to the step and reach golf club variation, but there are some directional differences in the rotation involved. When we lunge forward, we rotate in more of a downward direction, which imitates the downswing of the golf swing. When we step back and rotate more upward, we are imitating the backswing. Moreover, we are still activating our lower body while focusing on balance and rotation.

Strengthening Exercises

After doing the warm-up routine, we can work on some strengthening exercises. Lower body and core strength are key to preventing and/or relieving injuries in your lower back.

You may have your own workout routine and it will vary depending on the sport you play but the ones I will cover are important regardless of your sport. If you don't already have these exercises in your workout routine, you may want to add them in as they are essential for helping prevent back injuries.

An important thing to note is the fact that the reps I have written for each exercise are the amount that I perform. You can adjust the number of reps based on your own ability or comfort level. Challenge yourself, but don't overdo it, and stop if you feel any pain.

Core Exercises: Dead bugs

Yet another exercise named after an animal. But dead…

- Step 1: Lie down on your back with your arms up in the air and your legs directly above your hips. Bend your legs at 90 degree angles (like a reverse table-top position).

- Step 2: Keeping your core tight, lower your right arm (over your head) and left leg until they are just above the ground.

- Step 3: Bring them back up to their starting position and alternate sides (do not go too fast).

Perform 8-12 reps per side. The important thing with this exercise is to keep your back from arching up. You can prevent this by tightening your core. A good way to think about this is pulling your navel in toward your spine. You can also place a towel under your lower back before you start, and have someone else try to pull the towel out from under you while you do the exercise. If they succeed in pulling the towel out, then that means your core is not tightened and you are not keeping your back pressed against the ground.

Alternating arm and leg:

This exercise is essentially the reverse of the dead bugs.

Step 1: Get on your hands and knees, making sure that your hands are directly below your shoulders and your knees are directly below your hips. Also, make sure that your back is perfectly flat, not arched or hunched.

Step 2: Raise your right arm and left leg until they are parallel to the ground. Lower them back to their starting position and alternate sides (do not go too fast). Perform 8-12 reps per side. Like the dead bugs, a common mistake with this exercise is arching or hunching your lower back while moving your arms and legs. Another common mistake is dropping/raising your hip or shoulder when moving instead of keeping everything level. However, these issues can all be solved by remembering to keep your core tight.

Bear Crawls (forward):

- Step 1: Start on your hands and knees in the table-top position of the alternating arm and leg exercise.

- Step 2: Lift your knees up off the ground, while maintaining the table-top position. You should immediately feel your core engage, and your shoulders may also feel some strain, which is normal.

- Step 3: "Crawl" forward by moving your right arm and left leg forward, then your left arm and right leg forward. You can think of this exercise like a more difficult variation of the alternating arm and leg exercise; the differences are that your knees are off the ground and instead of extending your arms and legs, you are crawling forward. Crawl slowly and deliberately. After taking each step, pause for a split second, then take the next step. Make sure that your shoulders and/or hips are not tilting to the side when you are crawling forward and backward. Also, when you begin to fatigue from this exercise, your head may drop down and your shoulders and back may hunch up. Try to keep your back as flat as possible, and keep your head level with your chest.

- Step 4: Once you have taken enough steps forward, begin crawling backward. Move your right arm and left leg backward, then your left arm and right leg, and so on.

Step 5: Take about 10 steps forward and 10 steps backward.

Bear crawls (sideways):

- Step 1: Start on your hands and knees in the table-top position.

- Step 2: Lift your knees up off the ground, just like how we did the forward bear crawls, making sure to keep your core engaged. Spread your arms farther apart so that they are wider than shoulder-width (I move each hand about 6 inches outward, though this distance may vary for you depending on your arm span, shoulder width, etc.).

- Step 3: Crawl sideways by lifting and moving your right hand towards your left hand (left hand stays planted) until your hands are back to shoulder-width apart, while simultaneously lifting and moving your left leg to the left, away from your right leg, until your feet are wider than hip-width. You should now be in a position where your hands are directly beneath your shoulders and your feet are wider than hip-width.

55

- Step 4: Move your left hand to the left, away from your right hand, while moving your right leg toward your left leg. Now you should be back to the starting position, with hands farther apart than shoulder-width and your legs at hip-width.

- Step 5: Once you have taken enough steps to the left, begin crawling to the right. It is the same movement, but you are now moving everything in the opposite direction. Like the forward bear crawls, make sure to keep your back flat and your shoulders and hips level when you move. Remember to pause for a second after each step so you are not going too fast.

Step 6: Take about 10 steps to the left and 10 steps to the right.

Anti-Rotation Walk-outs:

For this exercise, you will need a resistance band.

- Step 1: Anchor the resistance band on an unmoving object at about stomach-height. Stand with your shoulders parallel to the band.

- Step 2: Hold the free end of the band in front of you using both bands, and squat down a little for more control.

- Step 3: Starting with the band anchored to your left, engage your core and step to the right. The band will try to pull your upper body towards the left, so you need to keep your core engaged in order to keep your hands in front of you.

- Step 4: Continue taking steps out to the right until you can no longer keep the band from pulling you out of stance, then stop.

- Step 5: Step to the left, back towards the band. Continue to do so until you no longer feel resistance. Like the bear crawls, try to pause for a second after each step.

Step 6: Perform 5 sets of stepping away from and back to the band. Make sure to switch sides. This is a good anti-rotation exercise for core stability, which means that you are using your core to keep your body from being pulled away in different directions.

Lower Body Exercises:

Bridges:

- Step 1: Lie down on your back with your knees bent and your feet flat on the ground.

- Step 2: Tighten your core (bring your navel toward your spine).

- Step 3: Without arching your back, push through the heels of your feet to lift your hips up, creating a straight line from your knees to your shoulders.

Step 4: Hold for 3 seconds, then return to the starting position. Perform 10-20 reps.

Single leg bridges:

Step 1: Set up the same way as a regular bridge, then raise one leg up in the air while keeping the other down.

Step 2: Tighten your core.

Step 3: Without arching your back, push through the heel of the foot on the ground to lift your hips up, creating a straight line from your knee to your shoulders (keep the other leg raised).

Step 4: Hold for 3 seconds, then return to the starting position. Perform 10 reps per leg.

Monster Walks:

- Put a resistance band around your knees or ankles (the higher you put the band, the easier the exercise is, so choose based on your abilities).

- Step 1: Stand with your feet just wider than shoulder width (or even wider than that if you want to make the exercise harder). Bend your knees slightly to get into a quarter-squat position. The resistance band may cause your knees to tilt inward, so make sure to push outward against the band. Keep your body weight evenly distributed to both feet.

- Step 2: Walk forward by placing one foot forward, then the other, making sure to keep each leg from being pulled inward by the band. In your starting position, imagine that you are standing on two parallel lines. Your goal is to walk forward along those parallel lines, with each foot staying on its respective line. Once you have taken 10-20 steps, walk backward, still keeping your feet on those parallel lines. Try not to rotate your hips as you walk. Keep your hips facing forward the entire time.

Banded Lateral/Side Steps:

Put a resistance band around your knees or ankles (the higher you put the band, the easier the exercise is, so choose based on your abilities).

- Strep 1: Stand with your feet at shoulder width. Bend your knees slightly to get into a quarter-squat position. The resistance band may cause your knees to tilt inward, so make sure to push outward against the band. Keep your body weight evenly distributed to both feet.

- Step 2: Take your right foot and step sideways out to the right. Bring your left leg toward your right and back to your starting stance. Then, step out with the right again. Take 10-15 steps. When you have done enough reps to the right, switch to the left.

Lunges:

You can do this exercise with weights or without.

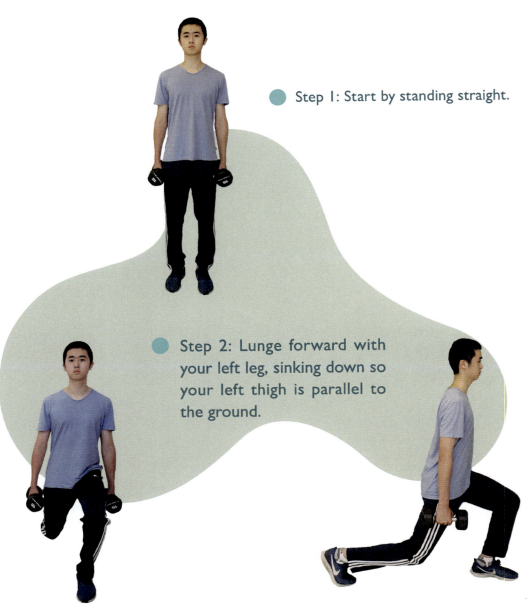

Step 1: Start by standing straight.

Step 2: Lunge forward with your left leg, sinking down so your left thigh is parallel to the ground.

- Step 3: Come back up to center and lunge with the other leg. When performing lunges, make sure that the knee of your lunging leg does not pass your toes because that will put excess stress on your knee.

- Step 4: Perform 10-15 reps per leg.

Creating a Schedule:

Now that we have covered some important exercises to help prevent injuries, we can look at when we do them and also the order we do them in. For most athletes there are three main cases for how you can apply these exercises. I will call them training days, workout days, and break days.

Training Days:

This is when you are practicing the sport you play. When you train for your sport, I recommend using this schedule as a guideline:

1. Start with foam rolling.

2. Go through your warm up routine. This will vary between sports so do whatever your personal warm-up routine is as well as some of the exercises under "Michael's Warm-Up Routine."

3. At this step you can start your practice.

4. When you are done practicing, spend some time stretching. During this time, do a few of the stretches from "Important Stretches."

5. Finish off with some more foam rolling.

Workout Days:

This is when you want to work out. You may want to spend a day just working out or you may want to work out and practice your sport on the same day. If the latter is what you are going for, just do both this routine and the one under "Training Days."

1. Start with foam rolling.

2. Go through your warm up routine. Once again, this will vary between sports, so perform your personal warm-up routine as well as some of the exercises under "Michael's Warm-Up Routine."

3. At this step you can begin your workout. Make sure to incorporate a few of the exercises from "Strengthening Exercises" into your workout.

4. When you are done working out, spend some time stretching. During this time, do a few of the stretches from "Important Stretches."

5. Finish off with some more foam rolling

Break Days:

These days are when you are taking a break: no practice or workouts, just relaxing. But it is still important to do some exercises, especially if you are taking a break because you injured yourself.

1. Start with foam rolling

2. Spend some time stretching. During this time, do a few of the stretches from "Important Stretches."

3. Go back to relaxing.

The Bottom Line...

That about wraps up the basic exercises you should perform to prevent back injuries. It really just comes down to stretching and working out a few muscles whenever you can (the stretching and strengthening exercises), doing a 10 to 15 minute routine before you work out or practice your sport, and spend around 10 minutes after exercising relaxing and loosening up (foam rolling).

There is no guaranteed way to prevent injuries, especially back injuries, but doing these simple exercises can greatly increase your chances of not needing to deal with them. If you do get hurt, these exercises are also a good way to help you feel better and recover. At the end of the day, you need to get stronger and more flexible in certain areas to prevent and/or recover from back injuries. You need to stay persistent with your training, but you also need to know your limits. Yes, it can be tedious, but consistently working on these exercises can help save you from a lifetime of pain.

Part 4: Golf Swing Faults

If you are wondering about how I messed up my back, this is the chapter for you. As a note, this chapter is specific to golf, so if you play any other sport, you don't need to read this chapter (but of course you are welcome to!). Also, everyone's golf swing is different, and although these points may not apply to everyone, they act as useful guidelines.

I'm going to show you what I did wrong and some major things you can avoid in your golf swing. Since it is uncertain exactly how my spondylolisthesis came to be, none of these points are definitive. After meeting with physical therapists and coaches, however, they agree on a few major points which I will discuss. Without further ado, here are a few things you want to avoid in your golf swing. This is not the complete list of the mistakes I made, but these are a few good examples.

One of the major causes of back injuries (including my own) in golf comes from incorrectly or inefficiently shifting your weight forward on the downswing. Here are some swing faults that suggest you are having trouble getting your weight forward and are doing something potentially harmful to your spine.

Swing Fault 1: The Front Leg is Not Posting Up at Impact

When you take the club up in your backswing, your weight shifts to your back foot (your right foot if you are right handed and your left foot if you are left handed). You could run into problems if you can't transition your weight to your front foot on your downswing. A good way to see if you are doing this properly is by checking if your front leg is posting up at impact or not. Posting up refers to the majority of your weight transitioning to your front leg as it rotates and straightens at impact.

As a general rule of thumb, when posting up while hitting an iron, a golfer's lead leg, including their lead hip, should be perpendicular to the ground. You should be able to draw a perfectly vertical line from the outside of your lead ankle all the way up to your lead hip.

A very important note to remember is that your lead hip must be against the vertical line drawn from the outside of your lead ankle, even if your lead leg is straightened. Many golfers (*cough* me *cough*) mistakenly assume that a straight lead leg indicates a proper post-up. However, if the lead leg is not perfectly perpendicular to the ground (as the line drawn indicates), then the golfer has not successfully transferred their weight. The exception to the rule above is the driver. When hitting a driver, you are hitting up on the ball as it is teed up, so golfers are actually allowed to stay behind the ball a little. As a result, your lead leg may be straightened and posting up, but not perfectly perpendicular to the ground. So, when you are checking your swing to see if you are correctly posting up, I recommend looking at an iron swing as opposed to a driver swing.

Looking at this picture of myself as a tiny little lad with a destructive swing, you can see that at impact, my front leg is not straightening up and rotating; rather, it is bent, and my knee is twisted outward. In general, golfers want to use their glutes, thighs, and hamstrings to rotate and pull themselves forward with their front leg. However, because my weight is on my back foot for so much of my swing, my left leg cannot do its job of posting up. Instead, my front leg is just bending, which results in my upper body falling backwards (what is known as "hanging back"), putting even more stress on my back. Make sure that this is something else you are watching out for in your own swing. Are you correctly shifting your weight forward to allow your front leg to post up and rotate?

Swing Fault 2: Back Foot Lifting Up Too Late

Another possible indicator that you aren't getting your weight forward is if your back heel is not lifting up at the right time.

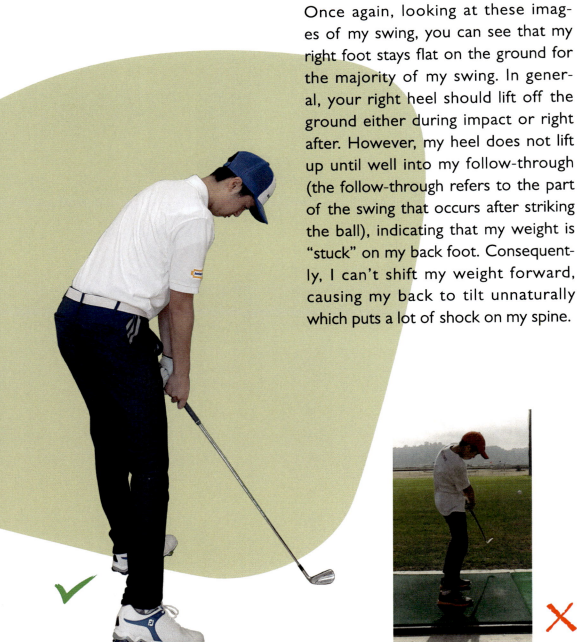

Once again, looking at these images of my swing, you can see that my right foot stays flat on the ground for the majority of my swing. In general, your right heel should lift off the ground either during impact or right after. However, my heel does not lift up until well into my follow-through (the follow-through refers to the part of the swing that occurs after striking the ball), indicating that my weight is "stuck" on my back foot. Consequently, I can't shift my weight forward, causing my back to tilt unnaturally which puts a lot of shock on my spine.

Swing Fault 3: Losing spine angle on downswing

The last main indicator of an improper weight shift that I want to address is losing your spine angle. Spine angle is the angle your head and rear create at address. This angle should be maintained until after impact. During the downswing, a common problem golfers have is standing up and out of their posture. This movement is very common, especially in young golfers. Most young players eventually get strong enough to maintain the correct spine angle. However, if left uncorrected for too long, this swing fault could be problematic for your back.

In some cases, loss of the spine angle is due to your weight being stuck on your back foot during the downswing. Consequently, you have to push off your back foot as hard as you can to get your weight onto your lead foot (as opposed to your lead foot pulling your body forward). However, the pushing motion can cause your hips to shift toward the ball while your head is pulled back away from the ball. Even then, your weight can still be predominantly on your back foot, causing an arching move that puts stress on your spine.

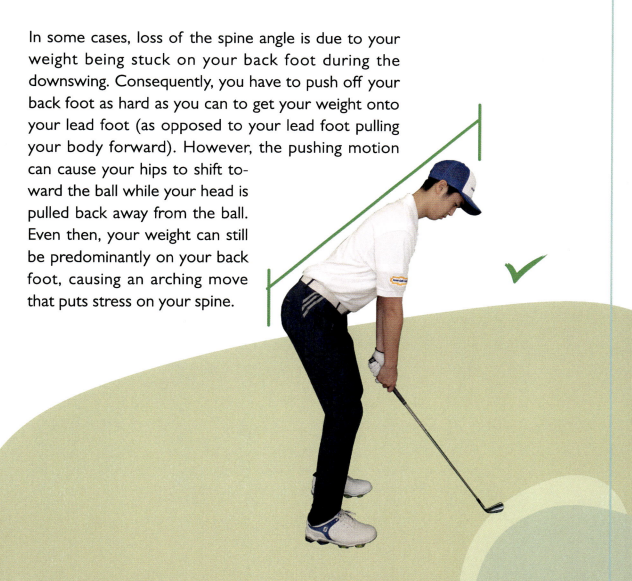

This mistake can once again be seen in my swing which is basically just "Three EASY ways to be mean to your spine!" In this picture where I'm addressing the ball, I've drawn a line in front of my head and a line behind my hips. Your head and rear should still match those lines at impact, which will help you strike the ball more consistently. However, notice that I've practically straightened up into a standing position, and my spine angle is virtually nonexistent.

So how do you fix these issues?

These three issues I mentioned all result from not being able to shift your weight forward. To get your weight forward, you should not only be pushing with your back foot, but even more importantly, you should be pulling your body forward with your front leg. However, if you are still having trouble with weight shift, a helpful drill you can do is the step-through drill. Set up with a club in your hands like you would normally do to address the golf ball, but stand with your feet together. Next, take the club to the top of your backswing, then stop. Finally, step down your target line with your left foot (if you're a right handed golfer) and swing. This drill will help you fix these harmful habits I discussed. It will help you pull forward with your front leg.

73

However, there are a few common mistakes with this drill. One of them is stepping and swinging at the same time, which will throw off your swing sequence. The key is when you are at the top of your backswing, you want to stay in that coiled position as you step forward with your left foot. Only once your left foot is planted do you allow yourself to swing through.

Another mistake is allowing your head to shift too far forward when you step with your left foot. When you perform the step-through move, make sure that you maintain your head position so that it is over or just behind where the ball would be.

Okay, so you've fixed the weight shift issue, but we're not done yet. If you remember back in "Swing Fault 3," I completely lose my spine angle during my downswing, which resulted in excess pressure on my spine. To fix this issue, put an alignment stick against your left glute when you are at address. Then, on the downswing, you need to keep your left glute on the alignment stick. To do so, instead of pushing off your right foot, you need to pull your left hip back toward the stick. Doing so will help you keep your hip in position and even help you post up on your front leg.

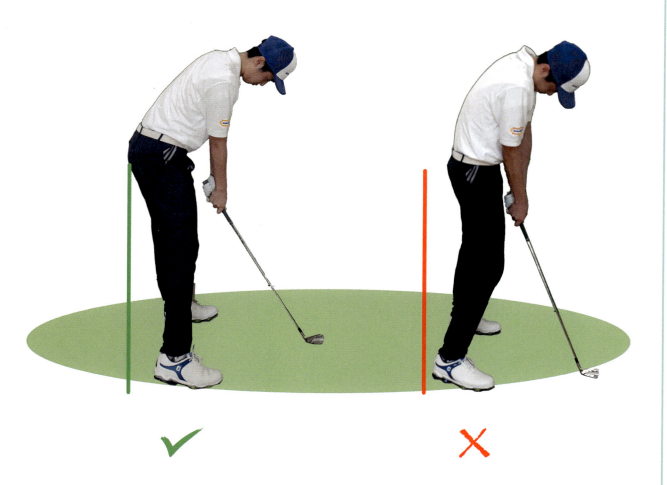

Part 5: Mental Game

Hi, this is Gerry, the protagonist's brother. Michael asked me to take complete control of this section and explain some things about the mental aspect of golf. I suspect that one day, long ago, the soon-to-be inventor of golf mused, "What can I do to frustrate people for generations to come? I know--I'll invent golf!" As an extra bonus to you, dear reader, here are some tips on the mental game in golf and many other non-contact sports. In the end, the most important aspect of it boils down to your ability to stay calm and cool under pressure.

Now, before we move on, Michael would like to emphasize that you can apply these tips to when you are injured. He says, and I quote, "Being injured can be extremely frustrating. When I hurt my back, I constantly felt restless and irritated because I wanted to go back to my normal routine of golfing and exercising. Instead, I had to 'take it easy' and rest. People all react differently to being injured, but we need to realize that patience is key. In golf, if you allow your frustration to get the better of you, a bad shot can lead to another or even a series of bad shots. Your round would be effectively ruined. The same idea applies to injuries. You need to keep your cool and be patient with yourself. If you allow frustration to get the better of you, you may rush back into playing your sport before being fully healed, and consequently worsen your injury. I have accumulated some tips with the help of my brother (who needs these a lot more than I do). He will explain them in detail." End quote. Here, golf is used as the main example, but they can easily be applied to other sports as well.

Anger/Frustration

Yep. We've all been there. Sometimes it just feels like no matter what you do, you can't hit the ball close to the pin, or the shot doesn't come out the way you planned, and it's all you can do to keep yourself from vigorously destroying every valuable object within a ten meter radius and then quitting. So how do we control our frustration on the golf course? Well, unfortunately, there is no definitive way to do so; even professional golfers occasionally lose their cool and break/snap/throw golf clubs. However, here are some tips that I find useful:

1. Take a Deep Breath

Ah, the classic. If you get angry on the course, taking a deep breath should be the first thing you do. It may sound obvious, but not that many players do this when they are upset. Taking a deep breath calms you down and helps prevent any angry outbursts. Not to mention, oxygen is mildly important for survival, so don't skip this step.

2. The Three-Second Rule

This is what I call the three-second rule. The idea is that you have three seconds to get mad and berate yourself about a bad shot. As soon as those three seconds have passed, however, you have to move on. The reason for this rule is that it can be difficult to control your anger, and holding it in for long periods of time can be near impossible for many people (such as yours truly). Keeping anger bottled up will only aggravate you more, so you need to vent your frustrations. However, you can't just explode as you will not only look like a complete psycho, but doing so will also ruin your focus and negatively affect your next shot. Moreover, your attitude can even negatively affect the overall mood of your group. Using the three-second rule allows you to blow off some steam while still maintaining your composure and focus. That being said, in those three seconds, there are still things you shouldn't do, such as cursing like a drunken sailor or snapping your club in half. You can, however, get mildly upset within that time frame and berate yourself a little. The important thing is that you need to keep your anger within those three seconds.

For example, when I'm frustrated or angry on the golf course after my ball follows Mcilroy's 3-iron at the Cadillac Championship and takes a swan dive into the water hazard, you might hear me say, "Wow, fantastic. You are truly high-quality garbage. What were you thinking, useless idiot? That was ju--oh my three seconds are up. Okay, I'm done. Moving on." And just like that, it's over. I find it especially important to tell myself that my time for throwing a tantrum is over because doing so puts the whole situation in perspective and I realize how stupid and ridiculous I'm being. That usually is enough to snap me out of my anger, and that is the whole point: don't snap your club, snap out of your anger instead.

3. Treat Yourself as Your Best Friend

Imagine that you are golfing with your best friend. They hit a bad shot, then proceed to disappear under a cloud of negativity and anger. How would you react? Obviously you would try to comfort and reassure them, right? (Unless you have a bet, I suppose. In that case, I would just smile smugly and say, "FOOL.") You would tell them that there's always the next shot, and that it's not a big deal, or something else along those lines. The same idea applies to yourself. Michael's coach always says that you have to "be your own best friend on the golf course." That is how you should act toward yourself when you don't play the way you are hoping to.

The next time you hit a bad shot, use the three-second rule to berate yourself if you have to, but then tell yourself, "Don't worry about it (insert your name here), you'll get the next one." Doing so will help you hit your next shot with confidence and positivity.

Nervousness

Golf is a nerve racking sport. When you are standing over that tricky shot that could make or break your round, you can really feel the pressure on you. Of course, being nervous will only negatively affect your game. So what can you do to stay calm?

1. Take a Deep Breath

Once again, taking a deep breath is very helpful, yet I find it is quite underutilized.

2. Practice Your Routine

This specific tip is a little more exclusive to golf as it requires a pre-shot routine. Practice makes perfect, and it is just as important to practice your routine along with your mechanics and other skills. It is crucial that your pre-shot routine is efficient and consistent. Oftentimes, when people are nervous, they take longer on their pre-shot routine. However, this is not a great habit as it means they are thinking too much and are messing up their usual rhythm. So, the solution? Practice your routine until it is muscle memory. In other words, you should be able to perform it exactly the same way each time, without actively thinking. Doing so will calm your nerves and provide something familiar for you to focus on, especially when under pressure. Moreover, it will also help prevent you from overthinking everything and standing over the ball for too long.

3. Don't Think About Your Score

I know that in tournaments, a lot of kids are always asking each other what score they are at, but I find that it is best to not think about your score at all. The reason is that it will only make you more nervous while playing because you begin to worry about your upcoming shots and the outcome of your round. Simply focus on visualizing your next shot. When you finish a hole, just write down your score and move on. It doesn't matter if the score was good or bad. It is just a number, and you do not need to let that number affect your emotions. If you've done this right, then you should not know what you shot until you tally up your score at the end of your round.

Reference books

Dr. Divot's Guide to Golf Injuries: A Handbook for Golf Injury Prevention and Treatment by Larry Foster

Golf Injury Handbook: Professional Advice for Amateur Athletes by Allan M. Levy and Mark L. Fuerst

The Physician's Golf Injury Desk Reference by Dr. Jeff Blanchard

Golf After 50: Playing Without Pain by Terry W. Hensle

Baseball Injuries: Case Studies, by Type, in the Major Leagues by W. Laurence Coker

Saving The Pitcher: Preventing Pitcher Injuries In Modern Baseball by Will Carrol

Pain Free Pitcher: Because Throwing a Baseball Doesn't Have to Hurt By Andy Powers

How I Play Golf by Tiger Woods

Golf My Way by Jack Nicklaus and Ken Bowden

Tennis Health: A Guide for Tennis Injury Prevention and Rehabilitation by Casey L. Deaton

Tennis Injury Handbook: Professional Advice for Amateur Athletes by Allan M. Levy and Mark L. Fuerst

Safe Tennis: How to Train and Play to Avoid Injury and Stay Healthy by Jim Martz

Golf Anatomy by Craig Davies and Vince DiSai

Complete Conditioning for Golf by Pete Draovitch and Ralph Simpson

All proceeds from this book will be donated to:

<u>North County Junior Golf Association</u>
<u>FC Heat/Escondido Soccer Club</u>
<u>Pro Kids, First Tee – San Diego</u>

These are all nonprofit organizations that provide opportunities for kids of all races and economic levels to participate in sports.

Made in the USA
Las Vegas, NV
13 January 2024

84271082R00055